Joy Comes in the Mourning

Finding Hope in the Hallway

Ray Lowe

ACKNOWLEDGMENTS

**First and foremost, I give all honor,
glory, and thanksgiving to God.**

For His endless mercy, His unfailing grace, His boundless
lovingkindness, and His patient hand upon my life.
He has never once given up on me, even when I stumbled
or lost my way. Every word written here is only possible
because of His goodness. Truly, *my story is for His glory.*

To my beautiful daughter, Melody

What a gift and joy it has been, as your earthly father,
to watch you grow and blossom into the remarkable
young woman you are today. You are intelligent, gifted,
compassionate, and strong. A true reflection of God's
handiwork. His daughter, His design, His delight.

I am so proud of the woman you have become. I can
only imagine how your Heavenly Father must smile over you
as He sees your heart for Him—and for others. I will forever
cherish the love, courage, and strength you poured into me
during one of the most difficult seasons of my life.
Thank you, Melody.

To my incredible son, Matt

It has been an equal honor to watch you grow into a strong, intelligent, loving young man whose heart beats to serve others. You live with humility, courage, and a quiet strength that inspires me daily. You are not only my son but also my brother in Christ. A servant-leader and a man who truly reflects the heart of God. In my hardest moments your courage and faith lifted me and reminded me to keep moving forward. I am so proud of the man you have become and for the example you set for those around you. Thank you for standing with me, Matt.

To Vicki

Though you are no longer here on this earth, your presence and your influence remain as strong as ever. You were not just a woman with a teaching degree—you were a born teacher, called and equipped by God to pour into others' lives. Even now, you continue to teach through the lessons you left behind, the memories you built, and the love you sowed so freely. I never fully realized the treasure I had in you until the day you left this world. And now—and every day since—I continue to discover just how rich a gift you were. Thank you, Vicki, for your legacy that lives on. Your faith, family, friendship, forgiveness, fun, and fortitude formed a foundation that will never fade. Though your voice is silent, your values still speak loudly.

To those who encouraged me to write

You believed in me when I struggled to believe in myself.
You reminded me that my words mattered, that my story had
value, and that it was worth sharing. Without your persistence,
encouragement, and gentle nudges, these pages might never
have been written. You saw a writer in me before I ever did.
Thank you for that priceless gift.

To Kelly Williams Hale

Kelly, you have been a true God-send on this journey.
Our meeting was no accident but a Divine appointment
and I am deeply grateful. From graphic design to editing,
from formatting to the countless behind-the-scenes details
that most will never see—you worked tirelessly to help
bring this book to life. Your faith, your creativity,
and your diligence made this possible.
Thank you, Kelly, for walking alongside me
and for making this dream a reality.

And finally, to each reader holding this book

Thank you for giving your time, your attention,
and your heart to these words. My prayer is that—
through these pages—you will see more of Him.
His mercy, His grace, and His unfailing love.

CONTENTS

PART II

INTRODUCTION

Grief is measured solely by the presence of an absence.

~ Ullie Kaye

Weeping may endure for a night,
but joy comes in the morning.

(Psalm 30:5 NKJV)

The Widows/Widowers Club is a unique group that no one wants to be a member of. Yet statistics show that there are 11.5 million widows in America today and 3.7 million widowers. An estimated 2,800 widows are added to the list every day (U.S. Census Bureau). If you are married, the likelihood of you and your spouse dying at the same time is very small. It's not the most pleasant thought. But most likely, in the future, you or your spouse will become a member of this club.

Grief is a process.

Grief is not meant to be a destination but rather a passage.

Someone once said, *"When God closes one door, He will open another . . . but it's hell in the hallway."*

Everyone finds themselves in a "hallway" at one time or another in life.

Unexpected events cause undeniable pain. A door suddenly, without warning, closes and locks, and you frantically run to the next door—only to find it also locked. In a panic, you run from one door to another, producing the same result: all locked. You stare down the hallway but nothing is in focus. Every door is a blur. You find yourself submerged in panic and anxiety. In a moment's time, the life that you had been enjoying now seems like years ago. Your past feels a lifetime removed.

If God is who He says He is, then why is this happening?

What kind of God would allow something like this to happen?

If there is a God then where is He?

When I need Him most, I find Him least.

This is not what I signed up for.

I can't understand this.

Hope is seldom noticed until it's gone.

Humans can live about forty days without food, about three days without water, about eight minutes without air, but only one second without hope.

When the door slams shut and you feel like you've been sucker-punched in the stomach and you're gasping for breath—what then?

Navigating the hallway can be both critical and challenging. The faith of your past now collides with the fear of your future. Next steps seem like they're a hundred miles away. The foundation that had held you so firmly in the past is now shaking and cracking. You sense your strength fading as you gaze into a fog. Days are long and nights seem like an eternity.

How can you make any decisions when you can barely make it through the day? Tomorrow doesn't exist—even in your mind. You aimlessly stare at a clock, as seconds turn to minutes, minutes to hours, and hours to days. Every day you become more aware that hope is slowly evaporating.

Why, God?
Why me?

Death, divorce, a devastating medical report, loss of a job, unexpected pregnancy, abuse, unforeseen events—life happens, and life suddenly turns.

Then what?

. . . .

A few years ago, I began journaling. It became therapeutic for me. It was not simply "trying to write something," but more like translating to paper the words I was hearing, the feelings I was sensing, and the emotions I was experiencing. Some days my posts were significant; other days, well . . . let's just say they were not as significant. From the journaling came a blog. And now from a blog comes a book.

This book details a journey that Vicki, my wife, and I took. Vicki was diagnosed with cancer in 2012 and transitioned to her Heavenly home on October 7, 2015. The first half of this book is devoted to Vicki's path with cancer. The second half is devoted to my path after her transition.

Please understand that sharing Vicki's path is from my perspective only. I realize that only those people who have personally heard the words, *"You have cancer,"* can fully comprehend what happens inside when you hear those words. I can't tell what she actually experienced and felt inside. I can only share her journey from my view beside her.

I will be open, honest, vulnerable, and transparent as I share my heart—especially in Part II—hoping that you will see God's goodness. This book makes no medical claims, nor do I claim to have found all the answers. Answers for cancer can be very elusive. This is simply our story.

My desire is that our story will provide you with hope . . . when life turns terribly wrong. My prayer is that when you find yourself in life's hallway you will discover the hope to get up . . . *one more day.* The hope to try . . . *one more time.* The hope to dream . . . *one more dream.*

*Hope is a good thing, maybe the best of things,
and no good thing ever dies.*

~ Andy Dufresne, The Shawshank Redemption

PART I

THE DREAM CLUNG TO ME WITH

A VIVIDNESS I COULDN'T IGNORE.

CHAPTER 1

THE DREAM

We are told that everyone dreams. Researchers have found that people usually experience several dreams each night. Some are able to recall vivid, almost cinematic details, while others wake with only a faint sense that something occurred in their sleep. For many, dreams vanish within moments of waking, like mist burned away by the morning sun.

My daughter, Melody, belongs to the rare group of dreamers whose minds produce elaborate, richly colored worlds at night. She amazes me with the intricate details she can recount—textures, sounds, conversations—as if she had visited another life while she slept. I have always been fascinated by people who have that gift, the ability to recall not just the storyline of a dream, but its fine brushstrokes.

I am not one of those people. Most mornings, my dreams slip away within the first hour, as if they never existed. On the rare occasions I remember one beyond a day, it's as if I've been handed a treasure.

. . . .

For years, I have begun each January with a 21-day Daniel Fast: no meats, no sweets, and no breads. It is my way of setting the tone for the year—preparing my heart and mind with intention rather than drifting into the months ahead. January 2012 was no different. On the eighth day of the month, I began my fast—expectant and hopeful for what the year might hold. New dreams, fresh goals, and Divine direction. I kept a journal during this time, recording what God was speaking to me.

Though I've surely had thousands of dreams in my life, I can count on one hand the ones that have stayed with me in full detail. But on January 13, 2012—day six of my fast—I had a dream unlike any other. It was the clearest, most concise dream I have ever experienced. Even now, more than a decade later, I have not had another like it.

When I woke, I knew instantly it was significant. The dream clung to me with a vividness I couldn't ignore. I didn't know what it meant, but I knew I had to write it down before the edges blurred.

This is the entry from my journal that morning:

> I had an unusual dream last night. I'm sure I dream most nights, but seldom do I remember them—this one stuck.
>
> I was in a waiting room of some kind, the sort you find in a medical facility. Time seemed to stretch on endlessly as I sat there, waiting, and watching. The room was full of people, each anticipating their turn to walk through a single door

at the far side. It appeared they were waiting for test results of some kind—lab work, perhaps.

I began to notice a pattern. One by one, people would walk through that door. Some looked nervous, others seemed relaxed, as though nothing serious could be waiting for them. But within minutes, each person returned, and almost without exception, they were devastated—sobbing, trembling, their faces pale with shock. It was heartbreaking to watch. I can still see the expressions—eyes wide with fear, shoulders bent under the weight of sudden hopelessness.

In the dream, I felt as though God Himself asked me, "What do you see?"

I answered, "I see people go in one way and come out completely broken—yet it all happens in just a few minutes."

Then I sensed Him asking, "Do you understand what's happening?"

The understanding came as if He spoke it directly into my mind: *In those few short minutes behind the door, nothing inside them has changed physically. Their bodies were exactly as they were when they walked in. But the words they heard have altered everything—not because of a physical change, but because of what was spoken over them.*

I realized in that moment the immense power of words. Words alone—without any change in reality—had the ability to dismantle hope and alter a person's entire outlook on life.

And then came the challenge: *If My people would believe My Word as much as they believe the words of medical personnel, their lives would never be the same.*

> **The words of man can bring devastation.**
> **The Words of God bring elevation.**

. . . .

That dream lingered with me for weeks. I kept turning it over in my mind, looking for its meaning. I had no connection for it. No immediate reason why God would show me such a scene except the reminder that I needed to trust His Word above every other.

By early March, springtime had begun to unfold like a gentle awakening as the trees and plants began to shake off the last remaining remnants of winter's chill and embrace the warmth and renewal of a new season. The air had a bit of crispness while carrying a hint of softness. A gentle whisper of the warmth to come.

Still, the trees—once bare and skeletal—had begun to adorn themselves in various shades of green. The flowers had taken on delicate blossoms of pinks, purples, and whites. It was as if the dull, brown landscape of winter had been transformed into a colorful preview of things to come.

There is an unmistakable energy as life bursts forth in every corner, from the smallest insect to the tallest tree.

Spring is in the air.

A season of hope and renewal, and the world is alive with endless possibilities.

It was during this month of new expectations and anticipation that Vicki discovered a small cyst. She had experienced similar things before and, each time, it eventually disappeared. We prayed in agreement, believing this would be no different. We trusted that the God who had handled it before would handle it again. After a few days, however, she decided to have it checked. Just to be certain.

She scheduled a mammogram for April 2. We expected routine results. After all, this was familiar territory. But almost immediately, the atmosphere shifted. The radiologist's expression darkened. He said he was "concerned" and recommended a biopsy. Before she left, he asked if she was a believer and told her he would be praying for her.

Vicki was visibly shaken. Later, she told me, "The words he spoke—and the way he looked—were so frightening."

She walked through that door into the waiting room, tears already spilling down her face. And then—just like in my dream—she was overcome, sobbing uncontrollably. She moved quickly to the car, desperate to escape the room, the eyes, and the whispers.

The scene unfolded exactly as I had seen it months earlier. It was a moment beyond déjà vu . . . more than just a similarity. I had been here before—in the dream God had given me—and now I understood.

That night, as we prepared for bed, I sat on the edge of the mattress, took Vicki's hands in mine, and told her there was something I needed to share. Until that moment, I had not told a soul about my January 13 dream.

I pulled my journal from the nightstand and read the entry aloud—word for word, exactly as it had been written. When I finished, we prayed together. We declared God's promises and spoke His peace over the situation. We came into agreement once again. We believed this was not too big for God.

> **For with God nothing shall be impossible.**
> (Luke 1:37 KJV)

"THE FIGHT WAS ABOUT TO BEGIN."

CHAPTER 2

THE DIAGNOSIS

"You have cancer."

Spoken once, but echoed hundreds of times in the chambers of the mind.

"You. Have. Cancer."

The devastation in those three words is unspeakable.

Words have power—and these are among the most potent ever uttered. They slice through the air and land like a verdict. Simply hearing them carries a weight of finality, as though a sentence has been passed. A terminal sentence. Fear rushes in like an uninvited intruder, gripping the heart, clouding the mind, and whispering its lies into the soul: *This is the end.*

Though we had never faced this particular enemy before, we were no strangers to battles. We had walked through valleys, fought other giants, and seen the hand of God move on our behalf. We knew enough of His Word to understand one truth with absolute clarity: fear does not come from Him.

> **"For God hath not given us the spirit of fear; but of power, and of love, and of a sound mind."**
>
> (2 Timothy 1:7 KJV)

And yet, knowing God's Word does not make us immune to human emotion. Those words, *"You have cancer,"* can pierce even the strongest heart.

Vicki and I had long been acquainted with the miraculous. Over the years, we had seen God's healing touch at work. First in our own lives, then in the lives of our children, and in countless others we had ministered to. We had a history with Him. A record of His faithfulness. We knew Him not merely through sermons or testimonies told by others, but through personal encounters. And because of those experiences, we carried a quiet confidence: *if God did it before, He could do it again.*

. . . .

Early in our marriage, Vicki began experiencing strange sensations in her head. Not quite pain. More like a sudden jolt or vibration, as she explained it, especially when she spoke. At first, it was sporadic. But gradually, it became more frequent and more troubling. Eventually, it began limiting her speech.

If you knew Vicki, you'd understand how remarkable that was. She loved conversation. Talking, laughing, and connecting with people was woven into her very nature. But as the months passed, she grew quieter, more withdrawn. This was not the Vicki I knew.

The situation became not only physically concerning but also emotionally draining. We prayed. We sought God. But the problem persisted.

Her journey for answers started with our local family doctor, then moved to specialists in Little Rock, Arkansas, and eventually to the Mayo Clinic in Jacksonville, Florida. She was examined by fifteen doctors over five years. Not one could give a definitive diagnosis.

Still, we prayed. Still, we believed. And still, nothing—at least nothing we could see—changed.

Vicki and I had been involved in ministry since the earliest days of our marriage. We wore many hats in the church: youth pastors, worship leaders, teachers, associate pastors, you name it. If there was a gap, we stepped in to fill it.

In 1989, a struggling congregation in our area approached us about becoming their pastors. The church had a reputation. Pastors didn't last long there. We knew the challenges going in. But despite that, we felt God's unmistakable call to step into that place. It was like a mandate!

We obeyed—and God met us there.

From the very first Sunday we walked in as pastors, the condition that had plagued Vicki for five long years disappeared. Just like that. Gone.

Five years. Fifteen doctors. No answers. Yet in one moment, completely healed.

Who, but God?

. . . .

Over the next several years, God's miraculous intervention became a recurring theme in our lives and in the life of our church. People were delivered from addictions, marriages were restored, oppression was broken. God moved in unmistakable, life-altering ways. It was a remarkable season!

In early 1995, Vicki discovered a swelling in her throat. At first, it seemed minor. But it grew—and kept growing—until it protruded from her neck, the size of a golf ball or more. She began dressing in high-necked blouses and turtlenecks to hide it.

Tests revealed something neither of us had ever heard of—a *thyroglossal cyst*. Benign in most cases, but occasionally cancerous, it needed to be surgically removed. The doctor strongly urged immediate action.

Vicki, however, wanted to pray first.

Months passed. The cyst remained. The turtlenecks continued.

Then came Christmas Eve. We piled into the car with the kids—as we did every year—to drive around and admire the lights. When we got home that evening, Vicki called me into the bedroom.

"I want to show you something," she said.

She pulled down the collar of her sweater. Her neck was perfectly smooth.

During the drive, she had reached up to touch the cyst—only to find it gone. Completely gone.

The next morning we gathered around our Christmas tree to open gifts. Vicki excitedly shared with our children the best gift she had received: the miraculous healing that she experienced.

We experienced firsthand miracles that only God could have made happen. Not just in Vicki's life, but in my life, in our children's lives, and in the lives of others.

These stories are not just memories—they are reminders. We knew the power of prayer. We knew the power of God's Word. We knew His ability to do the impossible.

We both thought this was simply a detour. Months later we would discover that this detour would become our destiny.

. . . .

"I'm sorry, but you have cancer."

Few sentences in the human language carry more force. They alter the air in the room. They pull time to a standstill. They shift reality in a single breath. Whether you are a believer or not, they unleash the same first wave: fear, dread, and the unshakable feeling that everything has changed.

After Vicki's diagnosis, we sat in the office of an oncologist. He spread out charts, explaining treatments, statistics, survival rates. His words were clinical but carried heavy implications.

"If you choose this treatment," he explained, "your survival rate is this percentage. If you choose that one, the odds shift slightly. Here are your options and this is my recommendation."

Vicki listened intently, then asked a question that stopped him mid-sentence:

"If I choose your recommended treatment . . . can you guarantee it will work?"

He looked her in the eyes, his voice steady but solemn.

"Ma'am . . . no one can guarantee anything."

She nodded slowly, then spoke with quiet resolve.

"I'll pray about it and let you know."

As we walked out of the oncologist's office that day, the late afternoon sun was sinking low, casting long shadows across the parking lot. It felt as though the world had gone strangely quiet—

like the moment before a storm when the air is thick. You know something is coming. You just can't yet see it.

We didn't speak much on the drive home. The charts. The percentages. The sterile explanations still echoed in my mind, clashing with the memories of miracles past. I knew God's faithfulness. I had witnessed His power with my own eyes. But now, faith was not a distant sermon—it was the only thing standing between us and despair.

For Vicki, the decision was never about statistics. She wasn't reckless. She simply believed that life-and-death choices must be made in the light of God's presence, not in the shadow of fear. She was determined to pray, to listen, to wait for His direction— even if the world told her time was running out.

· ·

That night, after the kids were asleep, we sat together in the living room. No words. Just her hand in mine. The weight of the moment pressed down, but so did something else—a quiet, unexplainable peace. We had faced the impossible before. We knew the sound of chains breaking. We had seen tumors vanish and bodies restored. And though the road ahead was dark, we also knew this: the same God who had been with us in every other battle would be with us in this one.

The fight was about to begin.

But so was the miracle.

**EACH PERSON MUST CHOOSE
THEIR OWN PATH.**

CHAPTER 3

THE DIRECTION

As humans, we are each wonderfully complex. We share many similarities, yet no two of us are exactly alike. Our fingerprints, our DNA, our life experiences—are all unique. As you read through this book, I want to make something crystal clear: the story I'm sharing is ours—Vicki's and mine. It's not a one-size-fits-all prescription for life. Each person must choose their own path. What worked for us may not be the way for you. I would never presume to say, *"This is the only road to take."*

However, I do believe with all my heart that every person should be aware of the alternatives and options available. They should seek out every piece of information possible before making life-changing decisions.

. . . .

Most people know the biblical story of David and Goliath. We tend to focus on the dramatic ending. David slinging a stone and felling the giant. But the beginning is equally important.

Goliath and the Philistines had stationed themselves on one side of a valley, facing Saul and the army of Israel on the other. For forty long days, Goliath emerged morning and evening to deliver his mocking challenge, intimidating the Israelites without lifting a sword. David's three oldest brothers were among Saul's soldiers.

Meanwhile, David was back home, tending his father's sheep—living his ordinary, faithful, unseen life. One day Jesse, David's father, told him to take food to his brothers. It strikes me as significant that Jesse could have sent any servant or another son, but he chose David.

David didn't volunteer. He didn't dream that morning, *Today I'll fight a giant.* In fact, the idea of battling Goliath was likely the furthest thing from his mind as he set out on that errand of obedience.

But when David saw Goliath's defiance and heard his insults, something rose up inside him—a boldness forged through years of quiet faithfulness. He remembered the lion and the bear he had faced while protecting his sheep. Those past victories had prepared him for the present challenge, and even for the future.

How we react to an attack will determine whether we step back or spring back.

When Vicki received her cancer diagnosis, I couldn't help but see the parallel. Just like David, she hadn't gone looking for a fight. She was simply walking in daily obedience, tending to life as usual, when suddenly—there stood her giant.

Cancer, like Goliath, came with an intimidating presence and a relentless voice. The medical reports, the statistics, the well-meaning warnings from others—all felt like that booming challenge echoing across the valley twice a day. It would have been easy to freeze. To feel powerless. To run.

But Vicki, like David, began to reach back into her own history with God. She remembered the "lions" and "bears" she had faced in her past. Seasons of hardship where God had carried her through. And with those memories came the courage to face this giant. Not in her own strength, but in the strength of the One who had never failed her.

On Thursday, April 19, we sat in a doctor's office for further testing. We prayed. We believed. But the doctor confirmed what we dreaded: cancer. An MRI was scheduled for April 27 to gather more information before deciding on treatment.

For Vicki, the reality was beginning to settle in—mentally, emotionally, and spiritually. On Wednesday, May 2, the doctor called with the results. There was a small lump in one of her breasts. We had already discussed possible treatment options in our earlier visit. Vicki told the doctor that we believed in the power of prayer and wanted to take time to seek God before making a decision. The doctor reassured us there was no urgency and to call once we had decided.

The diagnosis was now official. Vicki was standing in her own valley, facing the biggest giant of her life. She needed to hear—without question—the direction God had for her.

We had a spare bedroom that Vicki transformed into her meeting place with God. Morning after morning, she would close the door, open her Bible, and pour out her heart in prayer. Vicki was seeking God's voice above every other voice.

> **Her prayer: this interruption would become God's Divine intervention.**

Many people believe they have to follow the standard medical protocol for cancer treatment—without question. While serving on the Community Board of Mercy Ministries (now Mercy Multiplied), we met with Dr. Josh Axe—a chiropractor deeply knowledgeable in health and nutrition. He shared with us a natural protocol of diet and supplements that had benefited others facing cancer. We had another option.

Vicki began the plan immediately, while continuing to pray for God's guidance in every step.

Over the next several months, we immersed ourselves in learning. We researched, studied, and absorbed everything we could about the human body, nutrition, and alternative approaches to cancer treatment. It felt as though we had earned an unofficial degree in human biology, diet, and the complex causes and effects of disease.

The more we learned, the more amazed we became at God's design. The human body is a masterpiece, created with built-in mechanisms for healing. A simple cut is a testimony to this: you may clean and bandage it, but it's the body itself that seals the wound and restores the skin.

. . . .

The obvious path for Vicki was chemotherapy and radiation. But as she prayed, she felt more and more convinced that God was leading her in a different direction. She didn't yet know exactly where that path would lead—but she was certain it did not involve chemo or radiation.

On Thursday, May 10, Vicki met with the surgeon who had removed her gallbladder a year earlier. He was a man of faith, and she felt at ease with him. His recommendations were the same as before—a lumpectomy followed by treatment—but she still wanted to wait for God's peace before taking the next step.

We continued fasting and praying in unity. We stood on God's Word and reached out to every faith-filled believer we knew—pastors, evangelists, prophets, apostles, and teachers—asking them to join us in believing for a miracle. God's Word is true, and we held onto it with everything we had.

> *But even if the miracle didn't come as we hoped, we had already decided: we would not give up, give out, or give in.*

I FELT STRONGLY THAT MY ROLE WAS TO SUPPORT HER FULLY.

CHAPTER 4

THE DEVELOPMENT

The surgery was scheduled for Thursday, June 7, at 8:00 a.m. Vicki was at peace with the decision—ready to move forward. We had prayed, fasted, and called upon pastors and fellow believers to intercede. We stood on the promises of Scripture, spoke the Word over her, and filled our hearts and minds with it. Yet, the cancer remained.

We were deeply disappointed that the cyst had not been supernaturally removed. But having done all we knew to do, and recognizing that God often works through doctors, medical teams, and surgical procedures, we resolved to press on.

God's ways are not always clear to us.

Since the cancer was confined to one breast, Vicki chose to undergo a single mastectomy. Within just a couple of hours, the surgery was complete. In the doctor's own words, *"It couldn't have gone any better."* He successfully removed the cancer and a generous margin of surrounding tissue. Four lymph nodes were tested. They all came back negative.

In many cases, this procedure requires inserting a guide wire beforehand and placing a drainage tube afterward, but neither was needed in Vicki's case.

Praise the Lord!

Soon after returning to her hospital room, Vicki asked for food. They brought her a full meal, which she ate completely—and without a hint of nausea. Every detail of the day was a reminder to thank God. We were learning, once again, that He doesn't always move in the ways we expect or on the timetable we desire.

God is God, and we are not. He acts according to His wisdom, not our wishes. He does not require us to understand Him—only to trust Him. The cancer was gone, and Vicki felt an immense sense of relief to have this chapter behind her.

That night, after returning home, she took only a small portion of a single pain pill—and nothing after that. The following week, we met with the surgeon for her post-op checkup. All seemed well.

The next step was another appointment with an oncologist to discuss further treatment—chemotherapy, radiation, or both. Each option came with its own statistics and recurrence rates, carefully laid out in charts and percentages. But ultimately, the choice belonged to the patient.

Once again, Vicki turned to the Lord for direction. I felt strongly that my role was to support her fully in whatever decision she made. I was confident in her ability to hear God's voice and act in obedience to His Word. This was her decision. I was there to fully support her in whatever way she chose.

During that time of seeking God, she felt His guidance often through Scripture. One verse in particular became a cornerstone for her faith:

> *"And your ears shall hear a word behind you, saying, 'This is the way, walk in it,' when you turn to the right or when you turn to the left."*
>
> (Isaiah 30:21 ESV)

Vicki had also done extensive research by this point and understood that chemotherapy, while effective at killing cancer cells, is indiscriminate—it destroys healthy cells as well. Since she had radically changed her diet and was working hard to strengthen her immune system, the idea of introducing something that could weaken it was difficult for her to accept.

We had already planned a trip to California in early July to visit our son, Matt, for his birthday. We decided to postpone the oncologist appointment until after our return.

At the time, Matt was on staff at Free Chapel Orange County, a campus of Free Chapel in Gainesville, Georgia, pastored by Jentezen Franklin. The Orange County campus pastor was Javon

Ruff. During staff meetings, Matt had shared about Vicki's diagnosis and asked the church to pray.

While in California, I happened to pass by Pastor Javon's office and peeked in to say hello. He invited me in and asked how Vicki was doing. As I gave him an update, he suddenly paused mid-sentence and said, *"I've got something here that I'm supposed to give you."*

From his desk, he retrieved a book that a woman in his congregation had given him some time ago, telling him that one day someone would need it. He handed it to me, saying, *"This is for Vicki."*

The book was *Beating Cancer* by Dr. Francisco Contreras, founder of Oasis of Hope Hospital in Mexico, a world-renowned alternative cancer treatment center established by his father, Dr. Ernesto Contreras Sr., in 1963. Oasis of Hope had provided integrative cancer treatments for over 100,000 patients.

What Pastor Javon didn't realize was that, in our research, Vicki and I had already come across Dr. Contreras's work and were somewhat familiar with his approach.

Further investigation revealed that an extension of Oasis of Hope operated right there in Irvine, California, under Dr. Leigh Erin Connealy—a global leader in integrative and functional medicine, especially in cancer care. This facility later became known as the Cancer Center for Healing.

Dr. Connealy is the author of *The Cancer Revolution* (2017) and *Be Perfectly Healthy* (2009). She has dramatically reshaped the modern understanding of cancer treatment. In 2017, she was named one of the top 50 functional and integrative doctors in the United States.

TRUST REQUIRES WALKING WITHOUT KNOWING WHAT'S AROUND THE CORNER.

CHAPTER 5

THE DESIGN

When we arrived back home from California, there was a familiar quiet in the air. The kind that comes when the whirlwind pauses, and you know something new is about to begin. Vicki knew this season wasn't over. Another step waited ahead.

Up to now, her journey had been marked by a rhythm: one step at a time, never the whole staircase.

That's often how God works in the hardest seasons. He doesn't hand us a map from beginning to end. Instead, He lights a single stone on the path, asks us to step on it, and only then reveals the next.

For most of us, that's the hard part. We want the full picture. The timetable. The plan. The assurances. But trust requires walking without knowing what's around the corner.

This is not a medical manual, nor is it a promotion of any single cancer treatment. It is simply Vicki's story—one woman's walk through unknown territory, sharing the doors that opened for her and the choices she made. Every person's path is different, and each one must weigh their options prayerfully and carefully.

Her next date circled on the calendar was July 19: another appointment with the oncologist. We sat in his office under the bright, sterile lights as he began his presentation. His words were confident—too confident. He outlined his plan with precision: chemotherapy, radiation, pharmaceuticals—followed by more pharmaceuticals. Charts and statistics flickered across his screen, building the case for the standard medical association–approved approach.

But behind the polished delivery was a closed door. His posture left no room for questions. No space for discussion. The idea of alternative methods was met with the kind of polite dismissal that feels more like a shove. And yet, even as he declared his way the best way, he still admitted there were no guarantees.

Vicki listened quietly, her face calm. When he finished, she simply replied, "I'll give it full consideration and pray about it."

A few days later, her final medical report arrived. She filled out the forms for Oasis of Hope and scheduled a phone consultation.

On Monday, July 23, during her morning prayer, the words from Psalm 118:8 (KJV) came—clear, steady, and unshakable:

> **"It is better to trust in the Lord than**
> **to put confidence in man."**

That was her answer.

Her hope could not rest in human statistics or medical charts. It had to rest entirely in the God who had carried her this far. She remembered the words of 2 Timothy 1:7 (KJV):

> *"For God hath not given us the spirit of fear; but of power, and of love, and of a sound mind."*

Fear was no longer in the driver's seat. Faith was.

Oasis of Hope became the next stepping stone. The clinic was just twenty minutes from where Matt lived, so we could stay with him during the visit. The initial phone consultation confirmed what her spirit already knew: this was the path forward.

When the day came to meet Dr. Leigh Erin Connealy in person at the Cancer Center for Healing, Vicki walked through the doors with nervous anticipation. The building didn't feel like a typical medical facility. There was warmth in the air, worship music playing, and something almost intangible. Peace.

Dr. Connealy greeted us with kindness that matched her credentials. She wasn't just a physician. She was a woman who understood the marriage of science and faith. Dr. Connealy traveled the globe, speaking at conferences and learning the latest cancer innovations. She also prayed with her patients. She didn't just review Vicki's records—she looked her in the eye and spoke hope into her.

From that moment, Vicki felt the invisible weight of uncertainty lift. She was released into her next step.

The Cancer Center for Healing's philosophy was simple yet profound: cancer is not an isolated malfunction—it affects the whole person. Their approach was integrative, combining conventional medicine with advanced alternative therapies. They treated the body, the mind, and the spirit.

They didn't just ask, "How do we fight the tumor?" They also asked, "How do we restore the person?"

Dr. Connealy often quoted a powerful statistic:

> "An article published in the scientific journal *Pharmaceutical Research* suggests only 5 to 10 percent of all cancer cases are caused by genetic defects, whereas the remaining 90 to 95 percent may be caused by environmental and lifestyle factors—such as a poor diet, environmental pollutants, infections, stress, obesity, and physical inactivity. This suggests that we have the power to affect 90 to 95 percent of what causes cancer."
>
> ~ *The Cancer Revolution*

. . . .

With a care team now surrounding her, Vicki began with extensive lab work. The results set the course for her first phase of treatment: detoxification. The goal was to rid her body of toxins that could block healing. We stayed for several days while she began this process.

Over the following months, we returned periodically for targeted therapies: Ultraviolet Blood Irradiation, Hyperbaric Oxygen sessions, Infrared Sauna treatments, and Vitamin C infusions. Each one was chosen to strengthen her immune system so it could do what God had designed it to do—fight, restore, and protect.

This was more than a medical journey now.

For Vicki, it had become a walk of obedience—one step at a time, with faith leading and fear falling further behind.

THIS BATTLE WAS MORE THAN
PHYSICAL—IT WAS SPIRITUAL.

CHAPTER 6

THE DESIRE

The oncologist's words were clear and direct: there were no guarantees with the conventional cancer protocol. Vicki listened intently, but in her heart, she already knew. There were no guarantees with any alternative protocol either. Nothing about cancer was certain. Every path was a risk. Every choice came with unknowns.

It would take more than medical science. This was going to be a walk of faith—complete, total, and unwavering.

And so, Vicki made a decision. If she could not control the disease, she would control everything she could around it. She turned her life upside down—nutrition, exercise, rest, every part of her daily rhythm shifted. Gone were the carbs, the sugar, the processed foods. Every bite she ate was now deliberate and life-giving. The kitchen became her battleground and her sanctuary—organic greens piled on the counter, a juicer humming like a quiet declaration of war against disease.

When she prepared our meals, she'd ask what I wanted. At first, I was tempted to cling to my old habits. But I didn't want her cooking two separate dinners, so I began eating what she ate. I'll admit it . . . I felt like I was giving up too much at first. But slowly, something began to change. I noticed a lightness in my body and an energy I hadn't felt in years.

Within three months, I was hooked. My taste buds had surrendered to the new way of eating. I dropped twenty pounds. Vicki—miraculously—was back to her high school weight. We started walking 5Ks. Then running them. Her skin seemed to glow from the inside out. Vicki enjoyed a quality of life during this season that was beyond amazing. Exceeding anything she had hoped for.

And she would say, smiling with a strength that made people forget she was sick, "I may have cancer, but cancer does not have me."

At that time, we were both working as real estate agents. Vicki, ever private, never broadcast her illness. She didn't want clients wondering if she could handle the job. Even many of our coworkers had no idea. Outwardly, she looked vibrant. Healthy and unstoppable. Only a small handful of people knew the truth.

But not every day was triumphant. Some days felt endless. The weight of decision after decision—each one carrying the possibility of life or death—could be crushing. On those days, Vicki retreated to her "prayer room." It wasn't elaborate, but it was holy ground. She would close the door, fall to her knees—sometimes lying flat on the floor—and pour out her heart to God. She didn't just talk. She listened. And in that stillness, He spoke.

The answers didn't come as a grand map of the future, but as small, steady reassurances along the way. A whisper here. A confirmation there. Just enough light for the next step.

One afternoon, she emerged from her prayer time with a curious smile. "You're going to think I'm crazy," she said, "but while I was praying, I felt the Holy Spirit lifting me. Like I was being pulled upward. It reminded me of Star Trek." She grinned. "Beam me up."

A few days later, the three of us—Vicki, Melody, and I—were in a crowded shopping center, hunting for a parking spot. Out of nowhere, Vicki shouted, "Stop! Look!" I slammed the brakes and followed her gaze. In a sea of hundreds of cars, she was pointing at one license plate: **BMEUP 7**.

Her eyes were wide, her voice electric. "That's it! That's exactly what I felt in prayer—Beam me up! And look—the number seven. God's number."

To anyone else, it might have been a meaningless coincidence. But we knew better. The odds were absurd—finding that exact car, with that exact plate, in that exact place, at that exact moment. Impossible to explain away. I snapped a photo. It's on my phone to this day. Every time I see it, I'm reminded of how personally God cares for us.

Some call these "God winks." For Vicki, they were lifelines. Billboards. A stranger's passing comment. A lyric in the background at just the right moment. If you connected the dots, they formed a map of God's faithfulness. But you had to be willing to slow down and notice.

Too often, we race through life, blowing past the burning bushes God plants in our path. Moses could have done that in Exodus 3. But he didn't. He stopped. He turned aside. And when he did, he heard the voice of God.

That's what Vicki did. She stopped. She listened. And she heard Him.

Her next step came through research. She discovered Progressive Medical Center in Atlanta, Georgia—just a few hours from our home in Nashville. A place offering many of the same integrative treatments she had been receiving at the Cancer Center for Healing. She reached out, scheduled a consultation, and in January 2013, we drove down to meet Dr. Gez Agolli.

From the first conversation, she felt at peace. This was right. This was God's next provision. A care team was assigned, and treatments began.

Over the next months, we made trip after trip to Atlanta. Each time returning with new hope. Around that same period, she found a holistic doctor in Alabama whose therapies further strengthened her body. Every door God opened, she walked through—medical, nutritional, and spiritual.

We called pastors. We gathered believers. We asked for prayer, agreement, and a miracle. This battle was more than physical—it was spiritual. And Vicki, with her mix of grit and grace, fought it on every front.

HER FAITH WAS STEADY.

SHE WAS STILL BELIEVING.

CHAPTER 7

THE DESTINY

In the spring of 2015—March, maybe April—we made another trip to the Cancer Center for Healing in California. It had become part of our rhythm: travel west, run the blood work, track the cancer markers, listen to the doctor's counsel, and return home to keep walking the same tightrope between hope and reality.

A couple of weeks later, when the results came back, the doctor spoke with measured concern. The markers were up—elevated in a way that couldn't easily be explained. Still, her voice carried no alarm. Nothing in Vicki's regimen had changed, and she urged her to stay the course. *"If they're still elevated next time, we'll adjust,"* she said, her tone calm, almost casual.

In the weeks that followed, Vicki noticed she tired more quickly. She still lived her life—still smiled, still laughed—but I saw her resting more often, as though every hour needed a small pause to catch its breath. Within the small circle of friends and family who knew the truth, the same question came again and again: *"How are you doing?"* And she always answered with those same three words: *"I'm still believing."*

I had never seen anyone fight the way Vicki fought. It wasn't loud or dramatic—it was quiet, relentless, the kind of strength that doesn't need an audience. Her courage was unflinching. Her determination, unyielding. She didn't just endure; she moved forward.

Matt's wedding was set for June in California. We were in Nashville, but that didn't matter to Vicki. She worked from a distance, doing what she could to help, her heart fixed on one thing—she would be there. No matter what.

When the day came, she kept that promise. On June 5, under a soft California sky, Matt and Jenny said their vows. In the photos from that day, you would never guess the battle she was fighting. She looked radiant, beaming with pride. Those who didn't know her condition saw only the mother of the groom, healthy and happy.

When we returned home, the fatigue set in—heavy, unshakable. We told ourselves it was just the travel, the whirlwind of emotions. But as the days passed, Vicki withdrew a little more. Something wasn't right.

By July, the weariness had deepened. She began to ration her energy, choosing which tasks she could manage each day. August brought even more stillness; she became almost entirely homebound.

Her appetite began to fade. Food lost its taste. She forced herself to eat—small bites, sips of juice—because she knew nutrition mattered. It was one more act of defiance against the illness.

By September, she was mostly confined to the house. Her appetite waned further, her body weakened, and pain moved in like an unwelcome tenant—constant, sharp, unrelenting. Even walking from room to room became an ordeal. I asked, more than once, if she wanted to go to the hospital. Each time she refused, her voice steady but soft. She already knew what they would do, and she wasn't ready for that.

I think she sensed the end drawing near. But her faith was steady.

She was still believing.

· ·

On the morning of Saturday, October 3, I helped her to her chair in the living room. She was fragile now, her voice barely above a whisper.

"Do you want something to eat or drink?" I asked.
"No."

I made fresh juice anyway, hoping a few sips might give her strength. She couldn't take it.

Her pain was brutal—almost more than she could bear. This time, when I asked about the hospital, she said, *"Yes. I've got to have some relief."*

Our daughter, Melody, contacted a friend, an ER doctor at St. Thomas Hospital in Nashville. He was on duty and told us to bring Vicki in. When we arrived, they were ready for her. Within minutes she was on IV fluids, then admitted to a room. The goal was comfort now. Soon, she stopped speaking altogether.

On Sunday, the hospital doctor ordered scans.

Monday morning, he came back with the results. His words fell heavy in the room: *"The cancer has returned, very aggressive and spread so far . . . there's nothing more I can do except keep her comfortable."*

Hospice.

That was his recommendation.

By Tuesday afternoon, she was transferred to Alive Hospice in Nashville. The staff set up a bed for me so I could stay beside her. One nurse encouraged me to keep talking to her. *"Hearing is often the last sense to go,"* she said.

That night, a few friends came to pray with us. After they left, I pulled my chair close to her bed. Early in her journey, Vicki had memorized Psalm 91, reciting it often like a shield. I read it aloud now—slowly, letting each word hang in the air—then Psalm 23.

I was sure she heard me.

After reading, I began to pray, but the words came differently this time. Every prayer before had been for her healing here on earth. But now, my voice wavered as I said:

"Lord, I don't know what else to do. You love Vicki more than I ever could. She belonged to You before we began our life together. Tonight, I release her totally and completely to You. May Your will be done, and not mine."

As I laid down on the cot beside her bed I asked the night nurse to wake me if anything changed, if we needed to give her any medications. She seemed to be resting peaceably with no indication of any pain.

I drifted off to sleep. Around 1:00 a.m., I felt a gentle touch on my shoulder. Her voice was soft and gentle: *"Mr. Lowe, she's gone."*

Gone?
How?

I had been right beside her. I hadn't heard a sound.

The nurse, who had worked with hospice patients for many years, told me she could read the expressions on people's faces after they pass. She said, "Without a doubt, there was no pain, no stress, no struggle for her."

When I told her about reading the Scriptures and my prayer that I had prayed that evening, she said, *"No doubt she was just waiting between heaven and earth for direction. You gave her permission to go."*

And so she did.
Vicki got her direction.
And she went Home.

In the quiet that followed, the room felt impossibly still. Yet somehow, it wasn't empty. The air seemed to hold a trace of her. Her faith, her laughter, the fierce way she had lived. I could almost hear her voice, steady and sure: *"I'm still believing."* And I realized that her believing hadn't ended. It had only crossed a threshold. She had simply gone ahead. Where the pain was gone, the struggle over, and the promise complete.

IF I COULD JUST REMAIN CALM

AND BREATHE, THIS WOULD

END SOON, AND I'D WAKE UP.

CHAPTER 8

THE DISAPPOINTMENT

> *"Surely joy is withered away from the sons of men."*
> (Joel 1:12 NKJV)

The nurse asked if there was anything she could get for me.

Nothing at this point.

I sat on the side of the bed for what seemed like hours, though it was clearly only a few minutes. Dazed and disoriented, the room seemed to spin out of control. I tried to focus on something—anything—in the room, but nothing was stable. My heart was racing, and I struggled to breathe. I tried my best to compose my thoughts and get a grip, but to no avail. I was certain this was a dream—no, a nightmare.

If I could just remain calm and breathe, this would end soon, and I'd wake up.

Stay calm.
Take a deep breath.

Soon, I'll wake up.

The nurse quietly came to my side and tried her best to bring comfort. She asked if there was anyone she could call or anything she could get for me. Struggling to form a sentence, I told her I didn't think so. She softly slipped from the room, told me to take as much time as I needed, and gently closed the door.

Though silence filled the room, a thousand thoughts flooded my mind as the words kept echoing over and over: "Mr. Lowe, she's gone."

I tried to say something, but the words weren't there. Nothing would come out.

I was sure this wasn't reality, and at any moment, I would wake up and this horrible nightmare would be over.

This cannot be the way the story ends.

Broken-hearted and all alone, I sat for the next hour completely numb—hoping, expecting, waiting to wake from this nightmare.

My mind raced in a thousand directions. I wanted to cry. I wanted to scream. I wanted to speak.

I wanted to say anything. But I could not form a single sentence.

I wanted to pray, but who would I pray to? The God I had been praying to would never allow the story to end this way. I was sure He wouldn't.

What is happening?
"God, are You there?"

For the next five hours, it's difficult to put into words all the emotions that flooded my mind. As the clock slowly counted the seconds and minutes until dawn, I gradually realized I was not going to wake up—because I was already awake. I was being forced into a world I had no desire to live in, with no clue how to navigate it.

What do I do first?
What do I do next?
What about this?
What about that?

Throughout this journey, Vicki and I never discussed this ending. We both knew that no one gets out of this world alive, but this wasn't supposed to be the end. This was supposed to be a test— one that would become a testimony. A miraculous healing story of how God, at the last moment, raised her up to "live and not die, and declare the works of the Lord." This was going to be the greatest testimony we had ever experienced, and we would share her story with hundreds—maybe thousands—of people.

Perhaps you've made a mistake, God. After all I was supposed to go first.

Because we so strongly believed God was going to bring a miraculous healing, we never discussed any memorial service arrangements. Someday, we would—but not now. Not this time.

Throughout my life, I've prided myself on always having multiple plans: Plan A, Plan B, and sometimes even Plan C and D. But this time, there was no Plan B. This time, the only plan we both had was for God to bring healing on this earth. A miracle.

As darkness finally began to fade and dawn broke, I wish I could say reality set in but I'd be lying. Reality didn't set in. I was simply forced to proceed in this nightmare.

Questions had to be answered. Questions I had never even considered. Certain things had to be taken care of, so I stumbled through the immediate needs as best I could. With no prior arrangements in place, decisions had to be made quickly.

I had never done this before.

Where do I start?
Questions from hospice staff.
A funeral home had to be chosen.
Questions here.
Questions there.
Questions you don't think about until someone asks in a moment like this.
Arrangements had to begin.

Our son and daughter-in-law, Matt and Jenny, were in California, so dates for Vicki's service had to be carefully coordinated. Thankfully our daughter, Melody, was here to help with everything.

I will forever be deeply grateful and profoundly thankful for Melody. Throughout the entire process, she was an unwavering source of strength, solace, and support.

At that time, we had lived in the Nashville area for ten years and had many connections. Working in real estate, we had met a lot of people. Vicki and I were originally from Arkansas and had family and friends there as well. I realized that holding a service in only one state would mean many who wanted to attend would not be able to.

Melody and I met with the funeral director and discussed having two services—one in Tennessee and one in Arkansas. He assured us this was not unusual and that he would coordinate everything.

The first Celebration of Life service would be held in Franklin, Tennessee, on Friday, October 9. The second would be held in Heber Springs, Arkansas—Vicki's birthplace—on Saturday, October 10.

One service is difficult enough. Two services on two separate days—with a six-hour drive between them—was extremely challenging. But I realized it was necessary—to honor her. And to accommodate those who knew her.

Both services were planned as true celebrations of Vicki's life. A testimony of her time on this earth. The music and message were to be uplifting and offer hope to anyone who didn't have a personal relationship with God.

Because of the distance, I felt it best to choose two different pastors to conduct the services.

During Vicki's journey, we had connected with Pastor Larry and Doris Tomczak at a local church. For several weeks, we met on Wednesday evenings for prayer. Larry and Doris stood closely with Vicki throughout, and I asked Larry if he would speak at the service in Franklin.

On Friday, October 9, people came—and kept coming. The visitation line grew so long that eventually the funeral director told me they would have to curtail it due to time. The chapel was packed. It was overwhelming to see such a response. I knew Vicki was loved, but I had no idea just how many lives she had touched.

The service was filled with praise and worship and stories of Vicki's life.

Larry chose Ecclesiastes 7:1–4 (NKJV) as his text:

A good name is better than precious ointment,
And the day of death than the day of one's birth;
Better to go to the house of mourning
Than to go to the house of feasting,
For that is the end of all men;
And the living will take it to heart.
Sorrow is better than laughter,

For by a sad countenance the heart is made better.
The heart of the wise is in the house of mourning,
But the heart of fools is in the house of mirth.

A somewhat unusual passage, I thought, for a funeral—yet delivered with great depth. Not the typical scripture you'd expect, but very powerful.

That afternoon, we loaded the car and headed to Arkansas for the next day's service.

When Vicki and I married, we attended a small church pastored by our friends Millard and Virga Huett. Though they didn't live in Heber Springs, they had remained in Arkansas, and over the years, we stayed in touch. I asked Millard to speak at the service there.

Again, the service was a celebration filled with praise, worship, and stories of Vicki's life.

Again, the church was packed.

The impact of her life was astounding.

As the music ended, Millard stepped up to the podium and announced the scripture he had chosen: Ecclesiastes 7:1–4.

Really?
What are the odds?

It was such a strange, eerie feeling hearing the same passage read two days in a row.

There had been no consultation. Neither pastor had spoken with each other or knew what the other had planned. Yet both had chosen the same scripture. The sermons were different, but the scripture the same. It felt as if God Himself was bringing comfort —emphasizing those particular words through two different voices.

Both services ended with invitations for anyone who didn't yet know Christ to receive Him.

Family and friends gathered, shared stories, shed tears, and offered strength. Now the services were over.

Next came the short drive to the cemetery—a procession of cars winding slowly through familiar streets, each turn bringing us closer to the final goodbye.

At the graveside, a few final words were spoken—solemn, heartfelt, tender.

We stood in stillness as Vicki was gently laid to rest—the last note in a life that had touched so many.

Now the sun sagged low in the sky, casting its final golden sigh across the quiet cemetery. Shadows stretched long across the headstones, as if the earth itself was reaching out in grief. Leaves whispered in the hush, scattering across granite markers. Their brittle rustling a lament only the dead could fully understand. Sorrow clung to every breath like mist.

I stood for one final moment, feeling the darkness approach, and staring as a trail of car lights slowly disappeared from the gravesite. The wind tugged gently at my coat—like a memory refusing to let go. In my eyes, the last light of day flickered out—tender, broken, and endlessly waiting for a voice that would never call my name again.

PART II

" I FOUND MYSELF IN UNCHARTED WATERS—A PLACE UNKNOWN, UNWANTED, AND UNNERVING. "

CHAPTER 9

THE DEPRESSION

Time moves forward, yet sometimes life stands still.

Friends and family eventually return to their homes, slipping back into their "normal" routines. The world keeps spinning, days keep coming, and life presses on.

But my world had stopped.

The sunny skies turned stormy, the gentle breeze became a harsh wind, and the life I had imagined disappeared in an instant. I found myself in uncharted waters—a place unknown, unwanted, and unnerving.

How can I describe walking back into our home alone that first night? I still struggle to find the right words. The silence was deafening. At the same time the walls seemed to scream. To say I wasn't prepared would be the understatement of my life. I was beginning to understand that the world I had known—for so many years—would never exist in the same way again.

Welcome to my new reality.

The same house. The same bed. The same furnishings. But now, everything was different. It felt like being lost in a place entirely familiar. Everything looked the same, yet felt utterly foreign.

Every object a reminder that life had shifted in a way that could never be undone. It was like being lost in a place I once knew by heart—my own home now a stranger to me.

The days were long, but the nights stretched even longer. Tears came like tides, pulling me under when I thought I had steadied. Sleep eluded me; the darkness was too sharp, yet daylight was sharper still, cutting me with its insistence that life was moving forward when mine had stopped.

I reached out into emptiness, aching for a hand that no longer met mine, listening for a voice that would never again break the silence. I wanted to share the weight of this nightmare; to wake and discover it was only a passing storm, but instead I woke each day to absence that did not relent. The house was the same. The bed was the same. But the world—my world—had been unmade.

For anyone who has lost someone close, you understand what I mean when I say: *"The Firsts" are brutal.* The first birthday, the first holiday, the first change of seasons.

For me, it unfolded like this:

- Vicki passed on October 7

- Our wedding anniversary was November 17
- The following week was Thanksgiving
- Her birthday was December 1
- Christmas arrived three weeks later
- New Year's followed the next week

Within ninety days, I endured them all.

Every morning during those three months, I stood in front of the mirror and whispered to myself, *"I can do this. I can do this. I can do this."*

But on January 2, 2016, after surviving the gauntlet of firsts, I looked in that same mirror, shook my head, and said, *"I can't do this."*

It felt like I was sliding down a steep, slick slope into a deep, dark pit I had only ever heard others describe but never truly believed existed. The harder I tried to stop the fall, the faster I slipped. I reached out, desperate to grab hold of anything solid, something to anchor me. But there was nothing. No handholds, no footholds. Just the terrifying collapse.

Depression is real.

If you've never experienced it—or never watched someone you love endure it—I pray you never will. For the first time in my life, I understood why people in the grip of depression reach for drugs or alcohol. The pain is merciless, beyond reason, and the urge to escape—if only for a moment—is overwhelming.

My doctor offered to prescribe medication. But I was determined, at least for then, to try without it. Not out of judgment—if you've needed medication, there is no condemnation from me. Everyone fights their own battle in their own way.

One advantage I had was the foundation Vicki and I had built together through years of studying health and nutrition.

We are triune beings—body, mind, and spirit. Each part is distinct, yet deeply interconnected, feeding into and influencing the others. I knew if I could just force my body into motion—get up each morning, open the blinds to let in the sunlight, eat well, exercise, and rest—eventually, my body would begin to respond.

Discipline without depression is hard.

Discipline with depression is almost impossible.

Still, I committed.

For nearly two weeks, it was a daily battle.

- Yes, I have to get up.
- Yes, I have to open the blinds.
- Yes, I have to shower and get dressed.
- Yes, I have to move my body, even if only a short walk.
- Yes, I have to eat something healthy.

The next day—repeat.

By the end of the first week, the doctor's offer of medication sounded more and more inviting. Who would blame me? Who would even know?

I had never touched alcohol in my life, and I won't debate its use here. But the pain was so raw, so relentless, that I would have tried *anything* to make it stop.

Drugs. Alcohol. Anything.
Just make the pain stop.

If you've reached for those things in the middle of depression, I don't condemn you. I understand. The struggle is real.

For three weeks, I pushed through my daily routine. One day at a time—without numbing myself with any substances.

- *Get up.*
- *Open the blinds.*
- *Shower and dress.*
- *Exercise.*
- *Eat something healthy.*

And slowly, almost imperceptibly, something shifted.

Not a dramatic change. Not the end of grief, by any means. But enough to remind me I wasn't lost forever.

The darkness was still there but my eyes had begun to adjust.

" I ACCUSED HIM OF

ABANDONING ME IN THE MOMENT

I NEEDED HIM THE MOST. "

CHAPTER 10

THE DEVASTATION

Most married couples maintain separate jobs and lives outside the home. When one spouse passes away, the other often has the option of returning to work, pouring themselves into their job as both a distraction and a source of purpose.

Early in our marriage, Vicki and I lived that way. She taught school, and I worked in telecommunications. Life was busy, but it was also separate. We each had our own space, our own career, and our own rhythm.

But that all changed.

For the ten years leading up to her passing, Vicki and I worked side by side as realtors.

We truly lived and breathed the same air—24/7. We went to the office together, showed properties together, ran errands together, shopped for groceries together. You get the idea. We were inseparable.

Vicki handled the people and the paperwork, always ensuring

our clients felt informed and cared for. I focused on the driving, photographing listings, designing brochures, and managing most of the "tech" side of things.

She excelled at people skills. I excelled at technical skills.

Together, we balanced each other's strengths and weaknesses in a way that just worked.

On the rare occasion I went to the office without her, the first thing I heard was always the same question: *"Where's Vicki?"*

Where you saw one, you saw the other. Without realizing it, we had become very co-dependent. And when Vicki passed, I didn't just lose my spouse. I lost my business partner, my best friend, my confidant—my everything, or so it seemed.

I had learned to pray as a child, and prayer was a constant throughout my life. I had seen God move in supernatural ways more times than I could count. I had preached about prayer, taught about prayer, and prayed countless prayers that God had faithfully answered. But when Vicki transitioned from this life, my ability to pray was suddenly gone.

I was frustrated. I was bewildered. And yes, I was angry.

I had prayed every prayer I knew how to pray. I had pleaded, cried, begged, and declared. But when it was over, it felt as though none of it mattered.

Could I pray?

No.

Try as I might, it wasn't there anymore.

Angry?

Yes—angry.

I wish I could say that I handled it better. That I simply took a few days off and then got right back to life and faith as usual. Some people do.

Maybe you've lost a spouse or someone you deeply loved, and you found yourself able to lift your hands in worship, to praise God through the pain, to continue your relationship with Him as before. If that's your story, I admire you. May God bless you richly.

But that wasn't "my" story.

I was angry at a God who, from my perspective, had the power to heal Vicki but chose not to. A God who, though He loved her, let her slip away.

. . . .

As an earthly father, I knew if either of my children were at death's door and I had even the smallest chance to save them, I would do anything—*anything*—to keep them alive. So why wouldn't God?

So, no, I wasn't about to bow my head and pray again. Not after that.

Instead, I did something different. I began pulling up an empty chair in front of me and inviting God to sit down. I called these moments *"Conversations with God."* But truthfully, in the beginning they weren't conversations. They were monologues. I did all the talking, and I had a lot to say.

Other times, I remember pacing in our basement, yelling at God at the top of my lungs. I demanded to know where He was when I needed Him. I accused Him of abandoning me in the moment I needed Him most. I told Him exactly how I felt. Every raw, unfiltered emotion I had bottled up inside.

Why—when I needed Him the most— I found Him the least?

And then, when the shouting was over, I would apologize. Day after day, I would end with, *"God, I'm sorry. I know this isn't the right way to respond. Please forgive me."*

Until one day.

One day, in what I now recognize as a Divine appointment in our conversations, something shifted. As I was apologizing yet again, the monologue became a dialogue. In the quietness of that moment, I sensed God's voice saying to me: *"Stop apologizing.*

Don't apologize anymore."

But God . . . I thought.

Before I could finish the thought, He continued: *"I already knew your heart before you spoke a single word. And My love for you has not changed. Your yelling and your anger haven't altered My love in the slightest. Nothing you say or do will ever make Me love you more, and nothing you say or do will ever make Me love you less."*

Boom!

In that instant, for the first time in my life, I saw God in a completely different light. I felt His love—not as a reward for performance, but as a reality that existed no matter what.

. . . .

Growing up in church, I had subconsciously believed my relationship with God was tied to my performance. If I lived well, prayed hard, and did everything right, I could expect His blessings and His answers. But if I fell short, I thought I needed to earn my way back into His good graces by stringing together a few "good days."

That day changed everything.

It was as though God wrapped His arms around me and whispered: *"My love for you is not based on perfection, performance, or productivity. Whether you hit the bullseye or miss the target completely, My love never changes. It cannot increase. It cannot decrease. It simply is."*

That revelation lifted a weight I had been carrying for years.

> **It didn't give me a license to sin.**
> **It gave me the freedom to breathe.**

For the first time, I understood that God's love wasn't something I earned. It was something I could rest in.

And that realization has shaped everything since.

I FELT AS THOUGH I WAS TRAPPED IN A MAZE, EACH TURN LEADING TO ANOTHER DEAD END.

CHAPTER 11

THE DESOLATION

> *Hope is a very powerful force.*

It has been said that man can live for about forty days without food, perhaps three days without water, roughly eight minutes without air—but only for one second without hope.

In the days and weeks that followed, I felt myself caught in a relentless undertow of struggle and discouragement. Every step forward seemed to trigger an even greater slide backward—two steps ahead, only to be dragged three or four behind.

Hope, once a faint but steady glimmer on the horizon, began to dissolve into a slippery slope, always just beyond my reach. The harder I tried to grip it, the more it slid through my fingers, leaving me disappointed, disheartened, and drained by the exhausting effort to stay optimistic.

For most of my life, when storms came, I could ride them out. I would wrestle with disappointment for a few days, sort through the pain, and then move on. I assumed this time would be no different. I told myself I'd take a few days to breathe, process the grief, and then keep going.

Surely, that's how it would be.

And many well-meaning voices reassured me with their advice: *"You just need to get over it and get on with your life."*

Okay. That was my plan.

But plans are often the first things to crumble when reality presses in. As the days turned into weeks, and weeks into months, those intentions began to fade. Hope felt more like a shadow than a light, slipping further from my grasp with every passing day. I found myself wandering in a relentless search for answers that never seemed to come.

What had once been a steady flame guiding me through uncertainty began to flicker, sputter, and finally fade into darkness. In its place grew confusion, frustration, and a heavy ache in my spirit. The more I tried to make sense of what had happened, the more tangled the questions became. Each new one only added to the weight already pressing hard against my chest.

I wrestled with doubt.
I wrestled with disappointment.
I wrestled with discouragement.

I felt as though I was trapped in a maze, each turn leading to another dead end.

And somewhere in that labyrinth, the hope I once leaned on became a distant memory—something I could still recall, but no longer feel.

Very often when we find ourselves in situations that don't make sense, our hearts naturally long to ask God *"Why."* We wrestle with confusion, pain, and uncertainty, and it feels only human to bring our questions before Him.

Some people may say that we should never question God, as if our doubts or cries for understanding show a lack of faith. But the truth is, God is not intimidated by our questions. He is big enough to handle our honesty and gracious enough to meet us where we are.

Scripture shows us countless examples of people—Job, David, Habakkuk, even Jesus on the cross—crying out to God with raw, unfiltered questions. Their words were not met with rejection, but with God's presence and, at times, His gentle answers.

We may not always receive the explanations we were hoping for, but God never condemns us for asking. Instead, He invites us into a deeper trust. Sometimes His response is comfort rather than clarity, peace rather than pristine presentations. And in that process, our faith is stretched and strengthened.

Asking God is not a sign of weakness; it's a sign of relationship. It shows that we believe He cares, that He listens, and that He is involved in our lives—even when we don't understand what He's doing.

· ·

Grief has a way of reshaping not just the heart, but also the landscape of relationships. As with most married couples, so many of our friendships were built around shared dinners, trips, and gatherings with other couples.

There's a rhythm to that life—a natural pairing of stories, laughter, and connection that comes from being two halves within a community of twos. But when "we" becomes "me," that rhythm is broken. Suddenly, the dynamics shift, and the world you once fit so easily into feels foreign.

Other couples, even those with the best intentions, can struggle to relate. Conversations become halting, cautious. Invitations come less often, as though the absence of your partner is too heavy a reminder of life's fragility.

The calls and texts that once arrived so often begin to dwindle, and then fade. Friends become scarcer, and loneliness sets in—not just because of the loss of your loved one, but because of the quiet, secondary loss of the connections that once seemed secure.

Even my attempts to return to church, a place where I thought comfort and belonging might be waiting, left me feeling invisible and unseen. I sat in pews that once held us both, listening to songs we used to sing together, and instead of solace, I felt the weight of absence pressing in. People smiled politely, but their eyes seemed to slide past me.

It was as if grief had marked me in a way that made others uncomfortable, as though I carried something contagious. My sorrow felt like a disease no one wanted to risk catching, so they kept their distance.

What had once been a place of community became a reminder of how much my life had changed—and how much I no longer fit the mold of what others expected.

That sense of being contagious followed me everywhere. In conversations, people would rush to change the subject if I mentioned my loss, as if grief itself might cling to them. They found it difficult to mention her name.

In gatherings, laughter would sometimes soften when I walked into the room, as though joy and sorrow could not coexist.

I was not only grieving the absence of the one I loved, but also the shrinking circle of people willing to stand close enough to carry that grief with me.

That invisibility hurt almost as much as the silence of friends.

Church is supposed to be the place where the broken are carried, where sorrow is shared, and where no one walks alone. And yet, in my grief, I often felt more like an outsider than a member of the family of faith.

It's not that people were unkind. It was that they didn't know what to say, or feared saying the wrong thing, and so they said nothing at all. And in their silence, I felt not just unseen, but untouchable. As if my very presence was a reminder of the one thing no one wants to face: that loss can happen to anyone.

At one point, I even made a list of what not to say to someone who is grieving, because I had heard them all—the well-meaning platitudes, the tidy reassurances, the attempts to put grief on a timeline.

What I longed for was not a polished answer, but presence. Not solutions, but companionship.

> **Sometimes the holiest gift is simply to sit beside someone in their sorrow without trying to fix it.**

In the end, grief teaches a painful truth: loss reverberates far beyond the person who has died. It echoes into friendships, into the rhythms of daily life, and even into the very places where we once felt most at home.

And yet, within that ache lies a tender recognition—that love is at the root of all this pain, and that the God who sees what others avoid still holds space for every tear, even when people step back as though grief itself might spread.

. . . .

One day, in the quiet of my prayer time, I saw something—a vision. In my mind's eye, I was lying on a surgical table. Standing over me was what I knew to be God, His hands working deep inside my soul. My first reaction was to ask, *"Lord, what is this about?"*

In that moment, I felt His answer. There were things in my life— not necessarily sins, but weights, flaws, and patterns—that had quietly restricted me from becoming all He had created me to be. Attitudes. Pride. Arrogance. Selfishness. And the list went on.

That day, I prayed a dangerous prayer. That God would remove anything and everything from my life that displeased Him, no matter the cost.

And so, the process began.

It stretched over two, maybe three weeks. One by one, He began to remove those things. Layer after layer was stripped away until finally, I felt completely empty — exposed, bare, undone.

But emptiness was not the end.
It was the beginning.

Now, the rebuilding must begin.

Not a rebuilding of my own design, but His Divine design.

What was torn down was never meant to shatter me,
but to shape me. Never meant to crush me,
but to carve out space for something stronger.

What seemed like ruin was really a refining. Removing what was fragile, fleeting, and false, to make room for a hope that is firm, faithful, and forever. A hope not held hostage by circumstance but rather rooted in Him.

GRIEF—LIKE QUICKSAND—WAS

DRAWING MY FOCUS INWARD.

CHAPTER 12

THE DESPONDENCY

T he path of grief is not a straight road. It is uneven and full of moments when we are tempted to stop truly living and instead sink into a deep, consuming pit.

But who am I?

One of the greatest challenges we face after the loss of a spouse— whether through death or divorce—is the question of **identity**. Suddenly, the roles that once defined us shift, and we are left asking, *"Who am I now?"*

When you have shared your life with another person, your sense of self is often intertwined with theirs. You move through the world as part of a *"we"*—partners, companions, teammates. Then, in an instant, that identity is fractured. The "we" that shaped your days becomes "me," and the silence of that transition echoes in every corner of your life.

Embracing this new role is never easy. The absence magnifies the weight of rediscovering who you are apart from the relationship. This is especially true when the marriage was strong and enduring—when years, even decades, were spent building a shared life.

The role you played for your spouse—whether as nurturer, provider, confidant, or co-dreamer—no longer has a place to land. What once anchored you now leaves you adrift. And in that space of loss, the pressing question emerges:

"Who am I, now that I am no longer who I was with them?"

One of the most subtle of these dangers is the temptation to make grief entirely about ourselves. Without realizing it, we begin to turn inward, circling around our own pain, our own questions, and our own brokenness, searching for our new role.

I found myself slipping into that very place. My thoughts and prayers—once wider, fuller, and outward—became narrow and centered on me. Grief, like quicksand, was drawing my focus inward.

Before long, I realized that nearly every conversation I had with God had shifted toward myself:

God, why me?
Why is this happening to me?
What did I do wrong?
What will I do now?

Each question echoed louder than the last, and each one carried the same theme: *me.*

Then I was reminded of a scripture in 1 Samuel 16:1. After Saul's death, God asks Samuel, *"How long will you mourn for Saul?"*

That verse pierced me. It was as if God was whispering the same words to my heart: *How long will you stay here, circling around your own pain?*

It struck me—I wasn't only grieving Vicki anymore. I was grieving the loss of myself: my story, my future, my expectations. My sorrow had shifted from grieving over her to grieving over me.

This is something that often happens when we lose someone dear to us. In the beginning, the grief is sharp, raw, and focused on their absence. We mourn the empty seat at the table, the silence in the house, the unfinished conversations. We ache for the plans we had made together—the celebrations, the milestones, the little daily moments we thought were guaranteed.

> **A thousand moments I had taken for granted, mostly because I assumed there would be a thousand more.**

But as time stretches on, grief can slowly change shape. The sharp edges remain, but they turn inward. Without noticing, *we begin to grieve our own lives without them.* We grieve the version of ourselves that no longer exists, the future we will never know.

It's in that place where grief becomes dangerous—where sorrow turns inward and the focus becomes all about *me*.

. . . .

One day, in the midst of my endless questioning, I felt God break through the silence with words that startled me: *"This is not all about you."*

At first, I resisted.

Really?

But what about me?
What about my pain, my loss, my confusion?

That statement haunted me. I didn't realize it at the time, but grief had placed blinders on my vision. I was so focused on my pain that I had lost sight of God's presence, His purposes, and even His peace.

Lingering in that place—asking, pleading, demanding answers— can be exhausting. And it was. I spent days, weeks, even months in that cycle of questions, chasing explanations that never seemed to come. It felt like a one-sided monologue: me speaking, God silent.

Why?
Why?"
Why?"

But then, something shifted. One day—as I prayed the same questions yet again—the silence broke. I sensed God respond with a simple, almost startling answer: ***"Because I'm God and you're not."***

It wasn't the answer I was searching for. In fact, in earlier years, it might have offended me. My pride would have bristled. My heart would have resisted. But—in that moment—something inside me softened. Instead of anger, I felt clarity. It was as though a light had suddenly been turned on in a dark room.

And I found myself responding simply:
"You're right, God. You're God—and I am not."

That realization became a turning point. I didn't suddenly have all the answers. I didn't suddenly stop grieving. But I discovered something far more important: I didn't need to have *all* the answers.

Trust began to replace my questions. My focus began to shift— slowly, imperfectly, but undeniably. Instead of demanding explanations, I began to rest in the truth that God is God and I am not. That was enough.

. . . .

Looking back, I see now that grief had tried to trap me in myself. It tried to make me the center of my own story. But God gently reminded me that even in my sorrow, He is still at the center. My loss is real, my pain is real, but so is His presence—and His presence is greater.

That truth didn't erase the pain, but it reframed it. It lifted my eyes from the pit and gave me the strength to keep moving forward. Not away from Vicki's memory—but with it—carried in the light of God's unshakable truth.

TO LEARN, YOU MUST

CHOOSE TO BE TEACHABLE.

CHAPTER 13

THE DRIVE

Teach Me

The process of rebuilding slowly began to take shape. During my devotions one day, the Lord highlighted two scriptures from Psalm 25:

> *"Show me Your ways, O Lord;*
> *Teach me Your paths.*
> *Lead me in Your truth and teach me,*
> *For You are the God of my salvation;*
> *On You I wait all the day."*
>
> (Psalm 25:4–5 NKJV)

In a classroom setting, every student receives the same books, resources, and instruction. Yet not all students learn the same way, nor do they retain the same lessons. A teacher can do their best, but the student must possess a genuine desire to learn and apply what is taught.

As skilled as a teacher may be, they cannot make you learn. To learn, you must choose to be teachable.

Just as first grade prepares us for second grade, and second grade prepares us for third, I have become convinced that every experience in life is preparing us for the next step.

Life is a series of lessons—but we must decide whether or not we will learn them.

In high school and college, students take both required courses and electives. At the start of each new semester, there's a brief window of time when students have options: if the instructor isn't a good fit, if the material feels too difficult, or simply if they change their mind, they can "drop the course" without consequence.

Too often, we treat life's lessons the same way we treat electives. When the challenge feels overwhelming, we instinctively choose the easier path, opting to "drop the course" rather than push through.

But when we do, we risk missing the very lessons God desires to teach us.

Looking back, I can see that in some of my hardest seasons, God was trying to teach me something profound. Yet because the process was painful, I "dropped the class" before receiving what He intended for me to learn.

. . . .

Trust Me

> *"Trust in the Lord with all your heart,*
> *and do not lean on your own understanding."*
>
> (Proverbs 3:5 ESV)

Easy to say, much harder to live out.

As I was studying this scripture, a word that seemed so small suddenly became so large—**all**. *"With **all** my heart,"* led me to consider that there could be a level of trust that would be with less than my whole heart, or even varying degrees, or levels of trust.

I've noticed that our trust in others often depends on what I call the "3 W's"—What, When, and Way. We tend to trust people if they:

1. Do *what* we want them to do,
2. *When* we want them to do it, and
3. In the *way* we want it done.

If any of these expectations aren't met, our trust in them can quickly erode.

The same pattern can creep into our relationship with God. For me, God did not do *what* I wanted Him to do, *when* I wanted Him to do it, and in the *way* I wanted Him to do it. That forced me to confront a difficult question: *Do I really trust God?*

I wanted to, but I just didn't understand.

Newsflash: *It's okay to ask God questions.*

As I mentioned before, He is not intimidated by our questions.

From the time we are small children, well-meaning adults kneel down, look us in the eye, and ask with urgency, *"Do you understand me?"* When we enter school, that question follows us daily. Over and over again, we hear it: Do you understand me? This is our training. This becomes our life.

Our education—and the very process of learning as human beings—is built upon understanding. When something new is presented, the first question is always, "Do you understand?" If the answer is no, the teacher or instructor will try again, approaching from a different angle until the lightbulb finally comes on. Only then, when we understand, can we apply the knowledge being given to us.

From our earliest days—learning letters and numbers, building words from sounds, solving problems from figures—we lay down blocks of understanding. Those blocks become the foundation upon which all future knowledge rests. Reading, writing, shapes, colors, math, and logic. Everything is constructed upon what we first understood as children.

Understanding gives our minds a way to make sense of information and add it to our base of knowledge. Without understanding, nothing fits, nothing connects, nothing makes sense.

But what happens when life hands us something we cannot comprehend? The death of a child. The loss of a spouse. A job taken away. Tragedy striking our family or friends. In moments like these, we have no building blocks to rely on, no foundation to grasp. Our minds reach for understanding—and come up empty. And so, like countless others before us, we cry out to God: *"I just don't understand."*

If you haven't spoken those words yet, trust me, one day you will.

And yet, Scripture tells us: *"Trust in the Lord with all your heart, and do not lean on your own understanding."* But this is the opposite of everything we've been trained to do. From childhood, leaning on our understanding has been the very way we survive and reconcile what life throws at us.

When we understand something, it makes sense. When we don't, we tend to reject it, dismiss it, or wrestle endlessly with it. We *need* life to make sense. And yet, God does not always make sense.

Herein lies the struggle: *trusting God when we don't understand Him.* It is not natural. It is not easy. And there is no quick, three-step formula that makes it so. The only way to learn is through practice. Again and again and again. Perhaps that is why I was reminded once more:

When life doesn't make sense—***trust in the Lord.***
When I can't figure it out—***trust in the Lord.***
When I don't understand—***trust in the Lord.***

Transform Me

Transformation is never easy. To transform is to *undergo a thorough, even dramatic change in form, character, or perspective—to enter into metamorphosis.*

The apostle Paul reminds us:

> **"Do not be conformed to this world, but be transformed by the renewing of your mind, that you may prove what is that good and acceptable and perfect will of God."**
> (Romans 12:2 NKJV)

Notice Paul doesn't say *try harder* or *fix yourself.* He points us to a deeper truth: transformation is not the result of human striving but of Divine renewing. God is the One who reshapes us from the inside out.

Yet transformation always requires change, and change is rarely comfortable.

Change disrupts our patterns, challenges our assumptions, and forces us to confront pain we would rather avoid. Change requires surrender, and surrender often feels like struggle. Faced with this reality, many of us naturally gravitate toward the path of least resistance—the familiar road, the safe road, the road well-traveled.

Somewhere along my own journey, my perspective began to shift.

God revealed that I had a choice. I could withdraw from the grief course I was enrolled in—not literally, but spiritually. I could relocate, search for new employment, surround myself with new friendships, and attempt to build a life that felt untouched by loss.

Or, I could remain in His classroom—the sacred space where He promised to teach me lessons about grief that no book, counselor, or friend could ever fully impart.

The decision was mine.

· ·

With trembling faith and a deepening resolve, I chose to stay. I made a commitment before God. However long it would take, I would remain in His process. I would not rush ahead or look for shortcuts. I would sit under His instruction and learn everything He intended to teach me.

That choice did not remove the ache of loss. It did not erase the nights of tears or the days when I wondered if the heaviness would ever lift. But slowly, almost imperceptibly, God began to work. He met me in my questions. He steadied me in my doubts. He gave me glimpses of His presence in the very places I thought He was absent.

And so, my prayer was simple: **Teach me.**

His answer was steady: **Trust Me.**

And my heart shouted: **Transform me.**

This is the essence of transformation: a daily surrender, a willingness to remain in God's process even when it feels unbearable, and a trust that His classroom, though difficult, leads to life.

· ·

Maybe you are standing at a similar crossroads today. Perhaps God is asking you to stay in a season you desperately want to escape, to remain in a lesson you never wanted to learn. Friend, you are not alone. The same God who invited me to trust Him is inviting you as well. His promise is not to make the road easy, but to walk with you on it. His purpose is not to leave you broken, but to reshape you for His glory.

Transformation is slow. It is costly. But it is also sacred. And on the other side of it, you will discover that the struggle was not wasted—because every step was held in His hands.

"
IT'S NOT ABOUT HOW HARD YOU GET HIT

IN LIFE, IT'S ABOUT HOW HARD YOU CAN

GET HIT AND KEEP MOVING FORWARD.

"

CHAPTER 14

THE DETERMINATION

My daily prayer became, *"Lord, teach me. Transform me."*

To my surprise, that's exactly what He began to do.

Determination can be defined as *firmness of purpose; resoluteness.*

At that time, I wasn't as firm in my purpose as I would later become, but I was resolved—and determined—to move forward with this teaching and transformation from the Lord.

One Sunday afternoon stands out vividly in my memory. To this day, it remains etched in my mind.

It was a hot summer day, the kind where the sun blazes down from a cloudless sky. The air was thick with humidity, the breeze barely noticeable. Still, I was determined to get a walk in that afternoon.

It seemed like just another ordinary Sunday—or so I thought. But that day became one I will never forget, for it was the day I met *Rocky.*

You may be familiar with the *Rocky* movie series. Sylvester Stallone stars as Rocky Balboa, a resilient fighter who overcomes tremendous obstacles to become a champion. The series became iconic—beginning with *Rocky,* followed by *Rocky II* through *Rocky V,* then *Rocky Balboa,* and finally *Creed.*

Well, that particular afternoon, I met Rocky. No, no, not Sylvester Stallone!

Allow me to explain.

If you're a walker or runner, you know it's wise to stay alert. Every now and then, you'll come across a dog that isn't leashed or doesn't respect its invisible fence.

As I walked along this Sunday afternoon, minding my own business, I noticed a tiny white dog running loose in the yard ahead.

I'm a huge dog lover, and given his size, I was fairly confident he posed no danger.

As I drew closer, a flurry of white fur and unbridled joy bounded straight toward me, with his whole-body wagging, his tail a blurry metronome of excitement. He was followed closely by his owner, a kind, elderly lady with a gentle smile that seemed to radiate a warmth as welcoming as the afternoon sun.

I bent down to pet him, and she said with a smile, "This is Rocky."

Now, you can name a dog anything you want, but based on appearance alone, this little guy didn't look ferocious—much less like a fighter. He was pure friendliness, rushing up to me as if we had known each other for years.

Then she said something I'll never forget.

Out of nowhere, she asked, "Do you know why I named him Rocky?"

Curious, I said, "No, why?"

She replied, "Do you remember what Rocky said? He said, *'It's not about how hard you get hit in life, it's about how hard you can get hit and keep moving forward.'* I named him Rocky to remind me of that. Not enough people realize this today."

As I continued my walk, her words lingered, echoing in my mind. They were not just heard, but felt.

Later, when I got back to the house, grabbed some cold water and began to cool down, I looked up the exact quote from *Rocky Balboa*. In a powerful scene with his son, Rocky says:

> *"Let me tell you something you already know. The world ain't all sunshine and rainbows. It's a very mean and nasty place, and I don't care how tough you are—it will beat you to your knees and keep you there permanently if you let it. You, me, or nobody is gonna hit as hard as life.*

But it ain't about how hard you hit. It's about how hard you can get hit and keep moving forward—how much you can take and keep moving forward. That's how winning is done!

Now, if you know what you're worth, then go out and get what you're worth. But you've got to be willing to take the hits—and not point fingers, saying you ain't where you want to be because of him, or her, or anybody. Cowards do that, and that ain't you. You're better than that!"

• •

As the sun began to set and the evening began to approach, I realized God had smiled on me that day. He had sent a random, sweet, silver-haired lady and a small, spunky, fluffy white dog named Rocky to deliver an unforgettable reminder. Although she didn't quote any Bible verses, or sing any spiritual songs, I got the message. The truth was loud and clear.

Life is hard, and sometimes the hits are painful. But no matter how tough it gets—take the hits, and keep moving forward, one step at a time.

Thank you, Lord. Right place. Right time.

> **Determination to never give up—
> that's how winning is done!**

I CLOSED MYSELF OFF FROM THE WORLD,
QUESTIONING WHETHER LIFE WAS
EVEN WORTH THE EFFORT.

CHAPTER 15

THE DIFFERENCE

Life is a journey—a road unlike any other.

It winds its way through towering mountains and deep valleys, over straight stretches where the way ahead is clear, and through crooked paths where each turn hides what comes next. Along the way there are bright sunny days filled with laughter and joy, and there are long stormy nights when hope feels like a distant memory. There are victories that make the soul soar, and there are defeats that bring us to our knees.

Seasons change. So does life.

And with every change comes a choice.

No one escapes this life untouched. Sooner or later, storms will come. Sometimes they roar in suddenly, catching us off guard; other times they creep in slowly, like clouds gathering on the horizon.

Death is not the only storm that shakes us to the core. Divorce, betrayal, the loss of health, the loss of dreams, deep disappointments—these too can break our hearts and alter the landscape of our lives forever.

Change is not always bad. In fact, it often brings new beginnings, unseen opportunities, and blessings disguised in unexpected wrapping. But no matter the nature of the change, there is always a decision to make: *Will I move forward, or will I remain where I am?*

When Vicki transitioned to her heavenly home, I was thrust into a season I had never wanted and could never have prepared for. In my wildest dreams, I could not have imagined the changes that were about to unfold in my life.

For days that blurred into weeks, and weeks that stretched into months, I battled a relentless storm inside me. Depression took root. Anxiety stalked my thoughts. Anger boiled beneath the surface. Bitterness seeped in like poison. I withdrew from people. I closed myself off from the world, questioning whether life was even worth the effort.

Then, one day, God spoke to me. Not in a booming voice from the heavens, but in a quiet, unmistakable whisper to my heart. Again, He reminded me of something I had nearly forgotten: **I had a choice.**

Grief, He told me, is a natural and necessary part of life. He understands grief. After all, His own Son wept at the tomb of His friend.

But grief was never meant to be our destination, or a permanent home. It is a valley to pass through, not a land to settle in. It only becomes our destination if we choose to live there.

That day, God made it clear: *As long as you are breathing, you have a purpose.*

He drew my attention to His words in Jeremiah 29:11. But this time, He asked me to insert my own name, to hear it as if He were speaking directly to me:

> **"For I know the plans I have for you, Ray," declares the Lord, "Plans to prosper you and not to harm you, plans to give you hope and a future, Ray."**
>
> ~ Jeremiah 29:11, RLV (Ray Lowe Version)

As I sat with those words, my mind drifted back over our 40+ years of marriage. God had been faithful through every season. The mountain highs and the valley lows.

The chapter of *Ray and Vicki* was a story overflowing with blessings, but that chapter had closed. The vows we had made had been fulfilled, and she had stepped into her eternal reward.

But I was still here. My season had changed, but His calling had not. From before the foundation of the world, He had known me. He had written a plan for my life. That plan had not been erased.

The next season would look different. My role would change. My responsibilities would shift. But for His purposes to be fulfilled in me, I had to make a decision—an intentional choice to step forward. No one else could make it for me. It was mine alone.

In that quiet, reflective moment, God reminded me of a song He had given me years earlier:

God had a purpose for the trials you faced today.
God had a reason for things working out that way.
If your load seems heavy and it seems you just can't stand,
God had a purpose for the trials you faced today.

. . . .

Looking back now, I see how differently my story could have unfolded. The path before me branched in many directions. Each choice I made held the power to alter my future entirely. A single decision could have led me deeper into despair, bitterness, or isolation. But by God's grace, He led me toward healing, hope, and a deeper relationship with Him than I had ever known.

I will forever cherish the gift of meeting Vicki, the blessing of walking beside her, and the years of love, laughter, and shared life that God gave us.

I will be forever grateful that when my foundation cracked and my faith wavered, God did not leave me in the rubble. He loved me back into His presence, into a new depth of relationship with Him—a place of peace, purpose, and promise that I never knew was possible.

Because in the end, seasons will change, storms will pass, and roads will twist and turn. But as long as there is breath in our lungs, there is a purpose for our lives.

And the choice will always be ours.

ON THE PATH I DIDN'T CHOOSE

I FOUND A GOD I DIDN'T KNOW.

CHAPTER 16

THE DECISION

> *To everything there is a season,*
> *A time for every purpose under heaven.*
>
> (Ecclesiastes 3:1 NKJV)

If you've made it this far, let me say a heartfelt *"thank you."*

Thank you for walking with me on this journey. The path I've traveled was not the path I would have chosen. But on the path I didn't choose I found a God I didn't know.

Could I have discovered this deeper relationship with Him another way?

Perhaps.

But I'll never know.

What I do know is this: yesterday ended last night at midnight. I can't go back and rewrite the past, but I can move forward and shape the future.

Looking back, there are things I might have done differently. But I can't live in *"What if."* I can't move forward staring in the rearview mirror.

I'm often asked, *"Do you regret not trying to convince Vicki to take a different path or pursue other treatment protocols?"*

For weeks, I wrestled with that question.

During our journey, we met many others walking the same difficult road with cancer. Some chose the standard path of chemotherapy and radiation; others pursued holistic or naturopathic approaches.

In the end, we saw people survive—and others pass away—no matter which path they had chosen. There were no guarantees.

Trying to live in the place called *"What if,"* is a realm where questions endlessly circle, where scenarios are replayed over and over—day after day, week after week, month after month, and sometimes even year after year. In this space, the mind searches, hoping for a different result, wondering if a better outcome might have come from a different choice.

What if I had done this?
What if I had not done that?
What if _____ *?* (Fill in the blank)

When life throws you a curve ball—a loss, a disappointment, a heartbreak—it's easy to retreat into *"What if."* The death of someone dear, the loss of a job, the unraveling of a relationship, the struggles of parenting, or simply the weight of everyday challenges can all draw you into that relentless questioning of the past.

You nurse and rehearse alternate endings, convinced that a single different decision could have changed everything. You process, analyze, and replay events in your mind, hoping to arrive at a better destination. And yet, the harder you search, the clearer it becomes. The answers to *"What if"* will never be fully known.

Living in the past is like carrying an anchor that keeps you from moving forward. You try to get on with your life, but inevitably the questions return. *"What if I had made a different choice?"*

The truth is, living in *"What if"* is draining. It robs the present moment, replacing peace with restlessness. Time slips away—moments, minutes, hours, days, months, even years—lost in pursuit of answers that will never come.

Those who live in the past die to the present.

Through this process, I've learned something vital: there is a world of difference between *happiness* and *joy*.

Happiness is what many spend a lifetime chasing, always convinced it lies just beyond the next milestone—another job, another relationship, another achievement. It becomes a distant goal, a shimmering mirage that always seems just out of reach.

Some pursue it in success, others in love, and still others in solitude—hoping to stumble upon it like a hidden treasure.

But here's the truth:

Happiness comes from happenstance. It's rooted in circumstances. You're happy if the sun shines, if you get that raise, or if you meet the love of your life. But those things shift and fade.

God, however, offers something greater.
A deeper promise.
It's called **joy**.

Joy is not circumstantial.
Joy is not fleeting.
Joy is eternal.

In the relentless pursuit of happiness, we sometimes overlook the small, seemingly insignificant things. The moments that bring us joy: the warmth of a sunrise, the sound of a baby's laughter, or the comfort of a kind word.

. . . .

Writing this book was not easy for me. I carried the outline and idea for years. I would start, then stop. Start, stop—again and again. It seemed that every time I started, I was forced to relive the pain and heartbreak. So, I kept delaying the process.

Then, at the end of 2023, I heard God whisper: *"It's time."*

I asked, *"Time for what?"*
He replied, *"It's time to share your story."*

And in that moment, I understood: this journey wasn't just about me. God showed me that someone coming behind me would need to hear this story—how I walked through it, how I survived it, and how this would become a survival guide for them. Someone would need to know they are not alone. That they, too, can make it through. That there is hope.

Maybe you know someone who needs this book.
Or maybe . . . that someone is you.

If it is, thank you for reading to the end.

If you're walking through a season of mourning, there is hope for you.

If the life you're living is not the life you planned, there is hope for you.

If you feel trapped in a dark hallway where every door is locked, there is hope for you.

My prayer for you is that somewhere in that dark, desolate, lonely hallway of locked doors, unexpected disappointments, and unfulfilled dreams—**your joy will come in the mourning**.

. . . .

I don't know your story, your loss, or your pain. But if even a single moment in these pages sparked a flicker of hope within you, then every word I poured into this was worth it.

This isn't just my story—it's *our* story.

People sometimes ask if I still miss Vicki.
Every single day.

But over time, the mourning has given way to memories—memories of joy, laughter, and love.

**Tears and time help fill the space,
but missing someone's presence is never erased.**

As Dr. Seuss once said: *"Sometimes you will never know the value of a moment until it becomes a memory."*

Sometimes it feels like a lifetime ago.
Sometimes it feels like yesterday.

Every time I see or talk to Melody or Matt, I'm reminded of Vicki. You see, she left a part of herself in them—not only for me, but for the world. I am so thankful that Vicki was willing to sacrifice her time, her energy, her career, and her dreams to be a mom. She loved being a mom to our children and laid a godly foundation in them. A foundation I continually reap the benefits of.

. . . .

Kingdoms come and go, but they don't last.
Before you know, the future is the past.
In spite of what's been lost or what's been gained,
We are living proof that love remains.
We all live, and we all die,
But the end is not goodbye.
The sun comes up, and seasons change,
And through it all, love remains.
An eternal burning flame.
Hope lives on.
And love remains.
~ *"Love Remains"* by Tom Douglas and Jim Daddario

> **"I will turn their mourning into joy,
> and give them comfort and joy for their sorrow."**
>
> (Jeremiah 31:13b BSB)

> **"Weeping may endure for a night,
> but joy comes in the morning."**
>
> (Psalm 30:5b NKJV)

Still Believing!

AFTERWORD

Grief is a natural, God-given emotion that we all experience at one time or another. Grief was not meant to be a destination but a process. We choose to navigate the process based on a number of factors including, but not limited to, our DNA, the way we were raised, our relationships, and our personal beliefs. It only becomes a destination if you choose.

The theory of grief and the reality of grief are two totally different things. And when we are facing grief head-on, only then can we truly understand the differences. Grief is not a sign of weakness or a lack of faith. Grief is the price we pay for love. Great love produces deep grief.

Early on in my process, I was told, "Time heals everything."

What I discovered is that times does *not* heal everything. But it does produce a distance. And distance affords manageability. When I came to understand that I would not "get over this," but I would get to the point that I could "manage" it, the load was lightened immensely.

Vicki's passing was the most difficult thing that I've ever had to face. But in my darkest hour, I found God's brightest light. And in that light, God allowed me to dream again. I realized that God still had a plan for my life.

For several months I've told numerous people that I'm not the same person. However, recently I sensed God asking me if I had really changed or had I just become aware of who I always was?

I've pondered this question for a while and honestly believe that God gave me the answer in the question. *I've just become aware of who I always was.*

Every morning when I wake up and realize that I have a pulse, I know that God has a purpose for my life. He is not finished with me yet. The dreams that He placed in my heart are still very much alive.

God placed a dream within each of us while we were in our mother's womb. If that dream has become dormant, displaced, or disarrayed, let me encourage you to awaken it. It's time to dream again.

You're not too old, and it's not too late.

Your identity was never meant to be established in another person.

The role you played in their life was important, but it was never the fullness of who you are. Roles shift as seasons change and that's okay. It's part of life's design.

Your true identity is unshakable.

Remember: *your identity is rooted in God and God alone.* In Him, you are whole, complete, and secure. No matter how your roles may change.

Every breath you take says that you have a **purpose**.

Every day you get out of bed, it says that God has a **plan** for your life.

Every time you look in the mirror, your image reminds you that God has a **place** for you.

You are God's masterpiece created in His likeness, destined for greatness.

If you are feeling stuck in the process of loss and can't seem to move forward, let me encourage you to awaken the dream that God has placed inside of you. The dream that you have covered up. The dream that you have hidden. That dream you thought died is still alive.

There is hope! If you're struggling with a loss of any type, the Lord will help you *release the past, reclaim the present,* and *redeem the future.*

1.   Release the past.

Yesterday ended last night at midnight. Whether it's someone's death, a divorce, or just a disappointment, turn it loose and let it go. You cannot go back and change the past. You can't move forward if you continue to look back.

2.   Reclaim the present.

When you got up this morning, you had a pulse. That means you have a purpose. Regardless of how broken you may feel—even shattered in a thousand pieces—God is a master restorer. He will restore your life if you give Him all the pieces. Yesterday is history, tomorrow is a mystery, and today is a gift. That's why it's called the present.

3.   Redeem the future.

Awaken your dreams. The dreams you have covered up, hidden in the background, or tried to forget. The dream you thought had died is still alive. You are the answer to someone's problem. Someone is waiting for you to unwrap the gifts God has given to you. The future belongs to those who believe.

When Vicki passed, I never used the phrase, *"I lost her."* How can you lose someone when you know exactly where they are? There was never a doubt in my mind about where Vicki went. Instead, I chose the word *"transition."* She didn't disappear—she simply transitioned to her new home.

I often caught myself saying, "She **was** so beautiful. She **was** so talented. She **was** so kind."

Then one day, I felt the Lord gently whisper to my heart: "Stop speaking of her in the past. She **is** more beautiful. She **is** more talented. She **is** more kind. Every wonderful attribute you cherished in her is now magnified many times over. She is more alive than ever."

Still Believing!

ABOUT THE AUTHOR

Ray Lowe is a purpose coach, author, speaker, hope-dealer, and real estate consultant. He is the creator of the *"Still Believing"* blog and has been a contributing author to two Amazon best-selling books: *Take Your Position: Restoration in the Body of Christ—Volume 2,* and *Unleashed: Rise Up and Roar—Volume 2.*

If you're seeking clarity in your career, improving personal relationships, or simply striving for personal growth, Ray is committed to supporting you every step of the way. There is hope. He lives in Nashville, Tennessee and is available for in-person or online coaching. Ray provides personalized guidance and actionable strategies that inspire lasting change.

Connect with Ray at **stillbelievingorg@gmail.com**,
visit **stillbelieving.org**, or via direct message at:

- Facebook.com/ray.lowe.33
- X.com/raylowe
- LinkedIn.com/in/raylowe1
- Instagram.com/raylowe1